SUCH APPETITE

MORENO VALLEY, CA, 2004–2006

CHARLIE WHITE

WITH POEMS BY STEPHANIE FORD

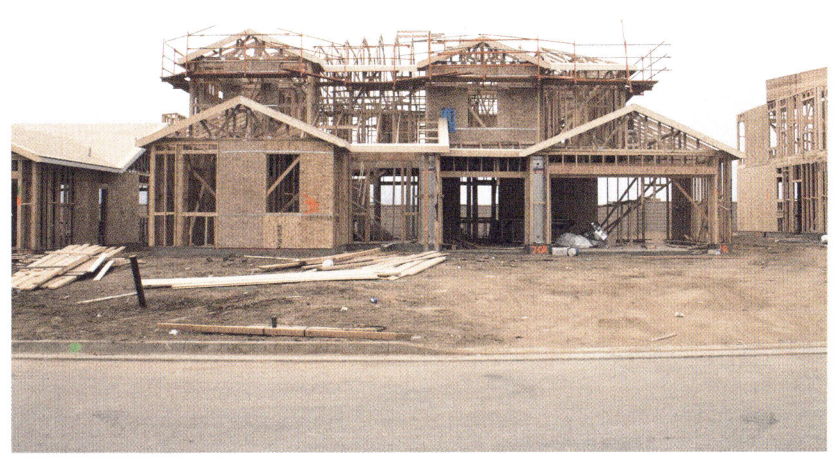

this is the story behind every
Mahogany-Type Distressed
with Rustic Knob and infinite hinge

we are the end or edge
of beginning again, meet me
at the holiday mall snow,

at the jacaranda seedpod
flattened by a skateboard,
at the name for breathing benzene

in a line of old cars with brand-new rims
our inching along is the local miracle,
heaven a candle called *Cinnamon Crisp*

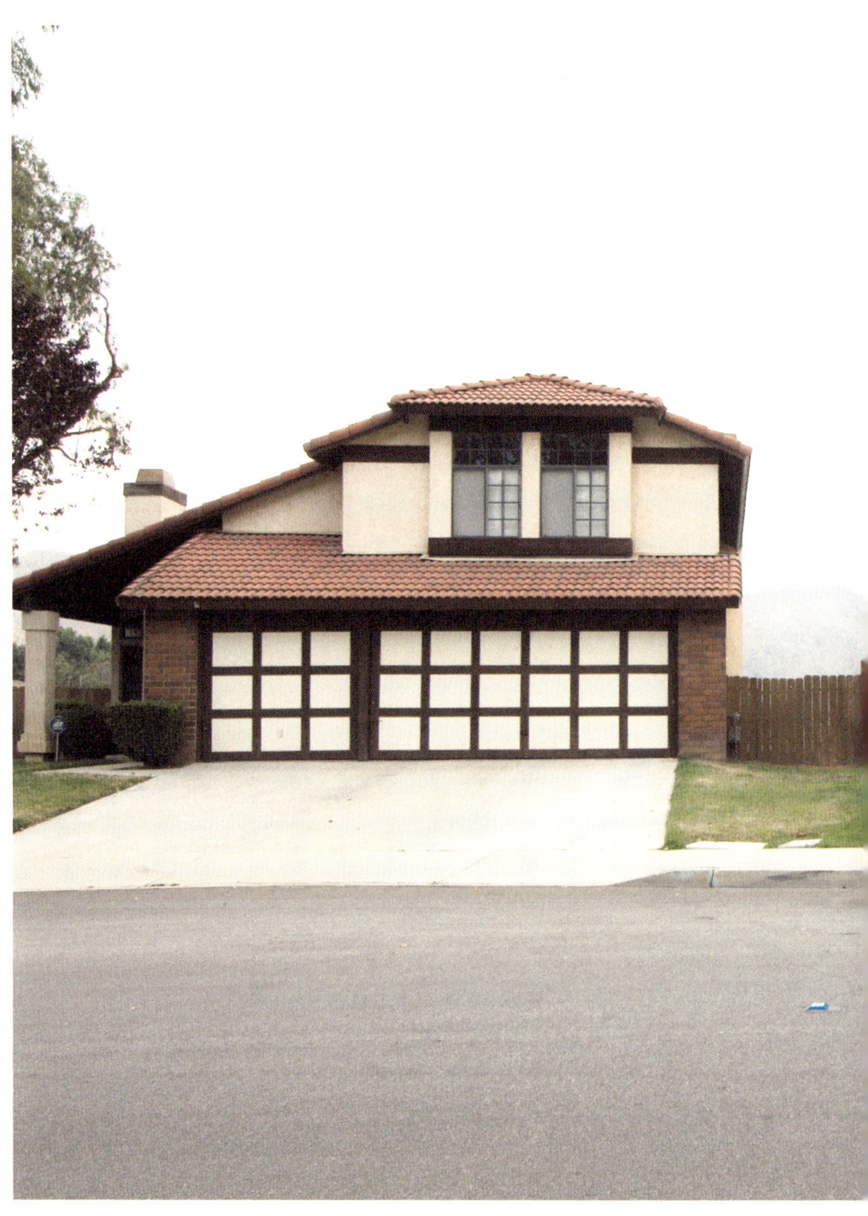

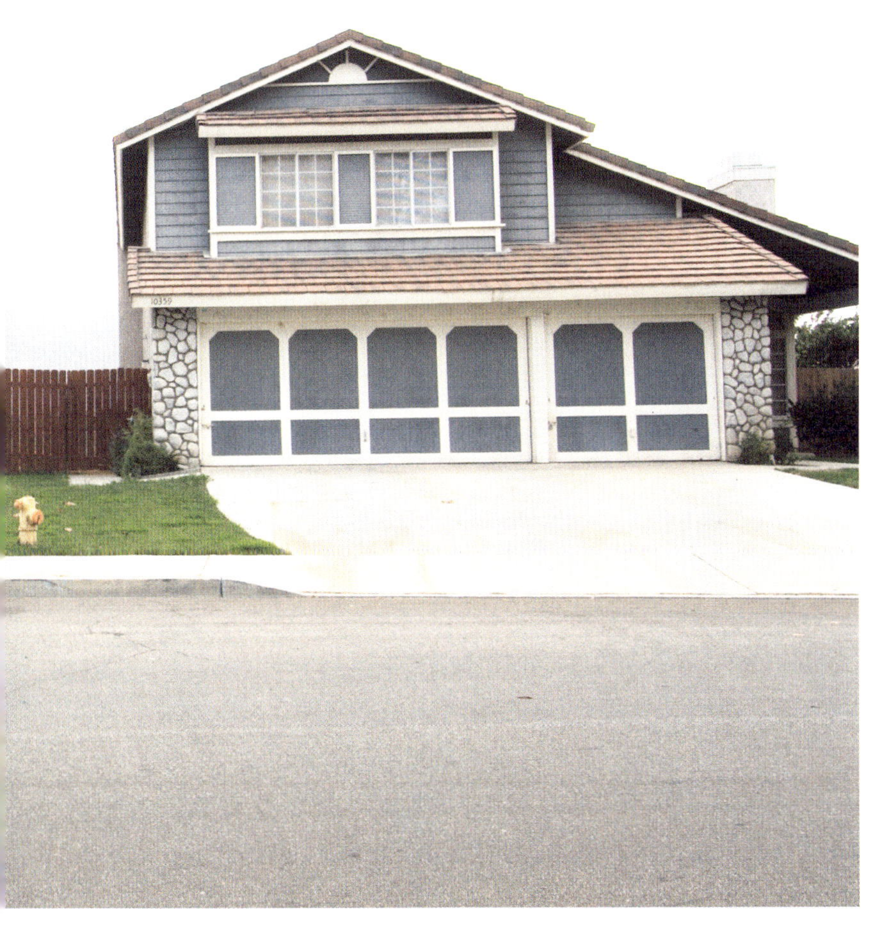
10359

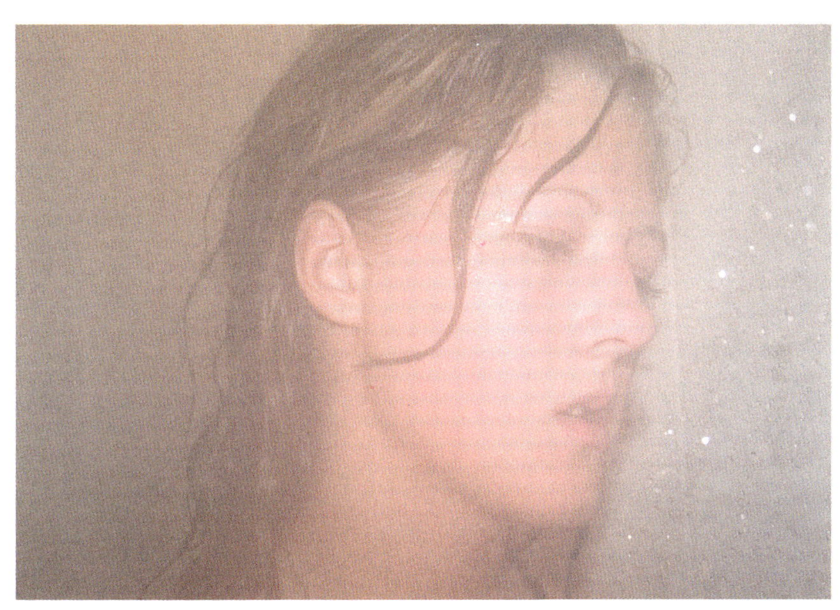

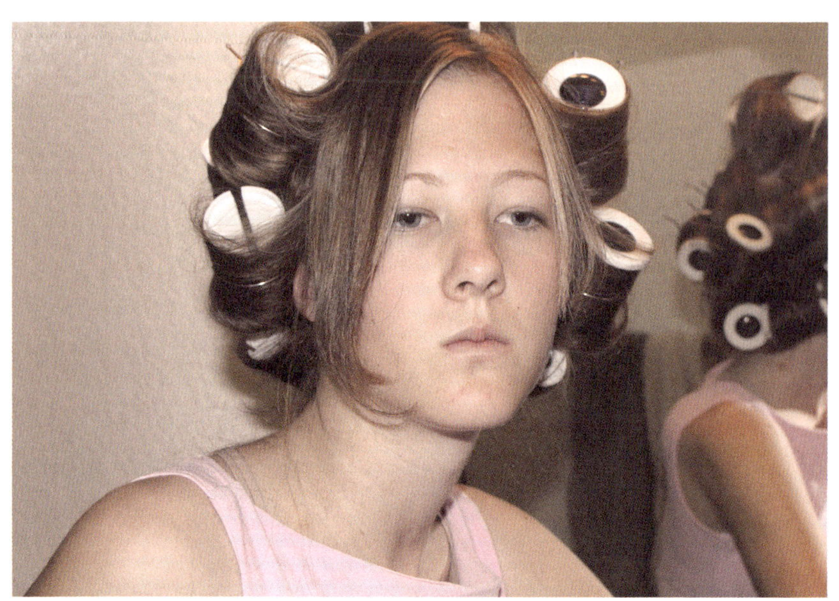

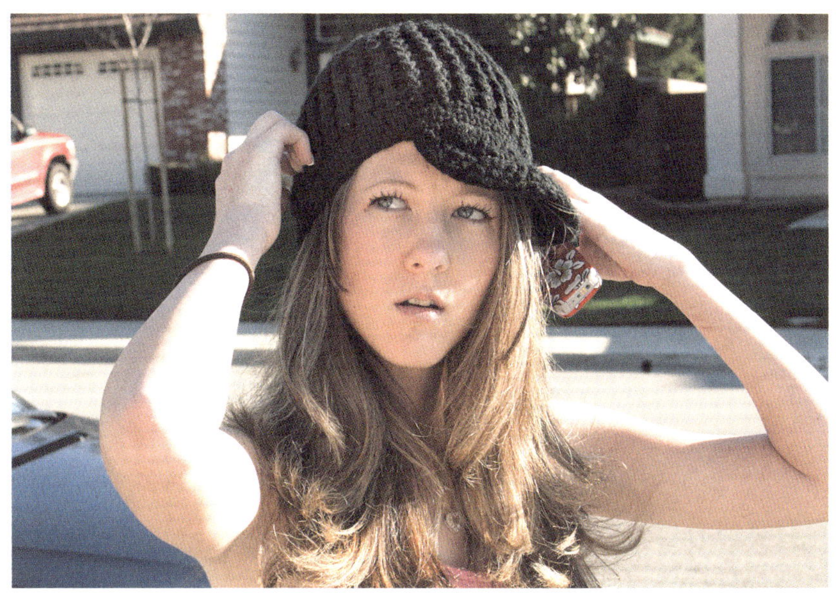

She, 15, slaps no means no
on apples serpents banishments.
She in every cuticle and lash
admired his adamantine physique
but saved her rep, cold-clocked him
in olive garden, stashes a bottle
of god in her locker,
swallows the whole of what she will,
salt and sweet at the all-you-can-eat.

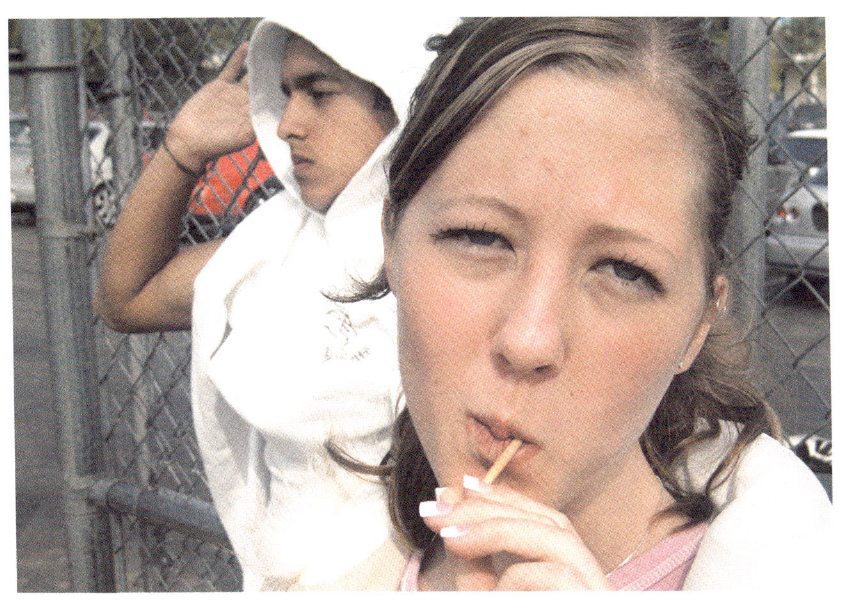

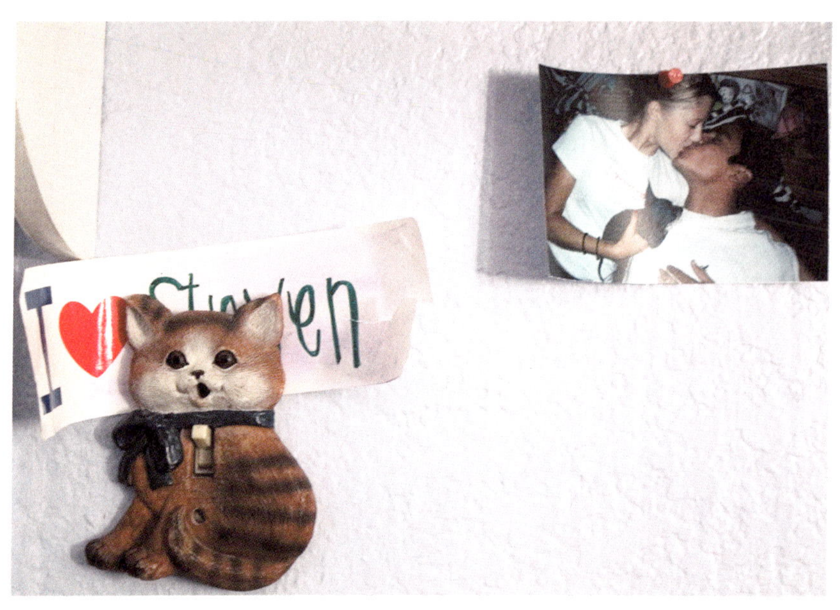

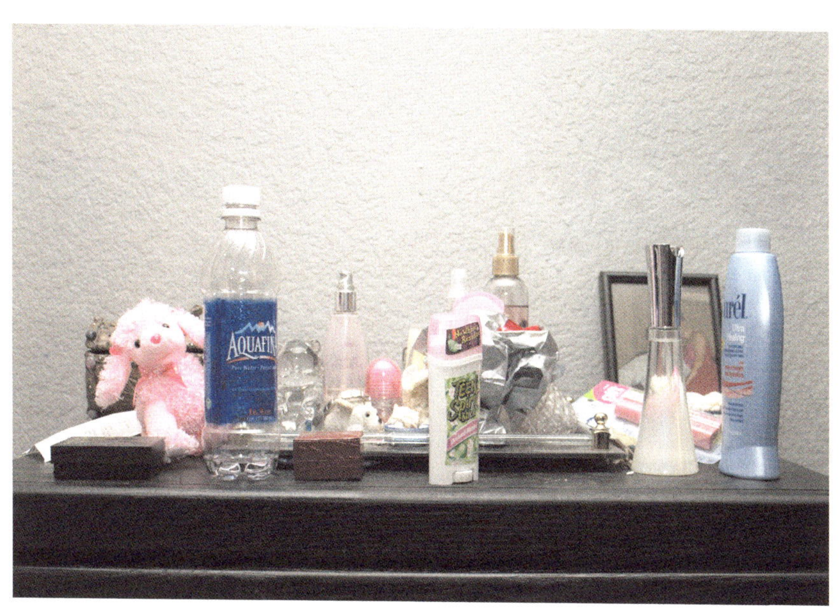

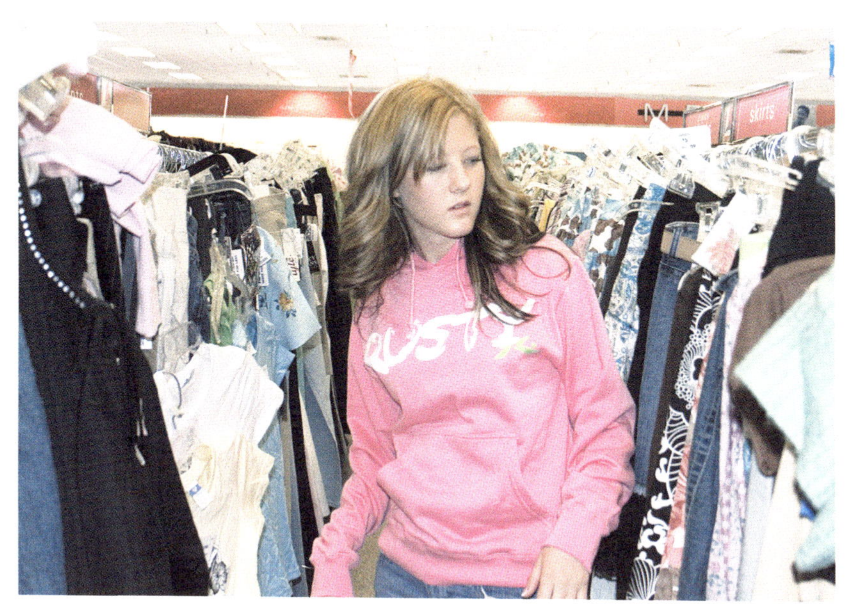
skirts

Youth is a machine of America,
glossy starving prayer we hum, forget,
set free to punch a register.

The future swallows all documents.
How else to live but scene by scene?
She was a good customer, she
guzzled our formula, such appetite
habit inherits a red planet
with piped-in everything.

What documents? It's all a riddle.
The earth was in-between civilizations.
Some boom-and-bust engineer came here,
'dozed the hunting ground open for business.

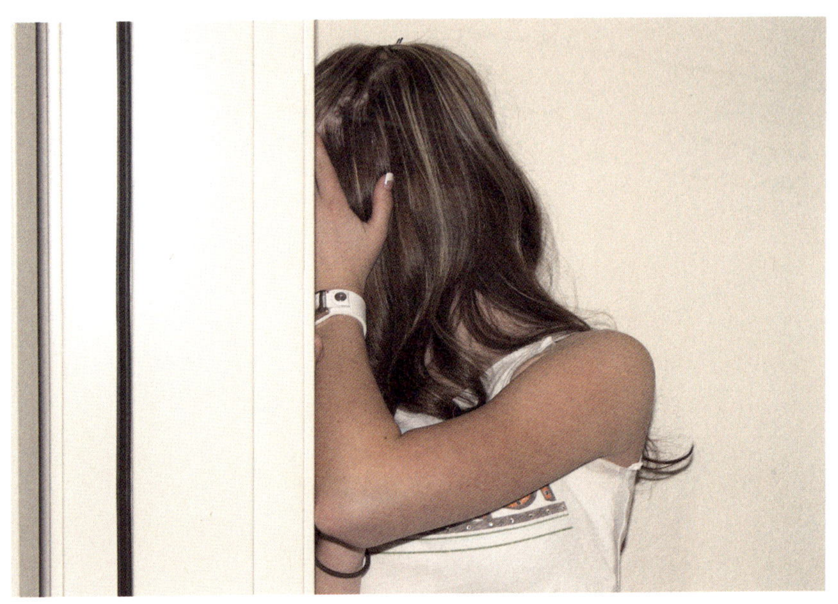

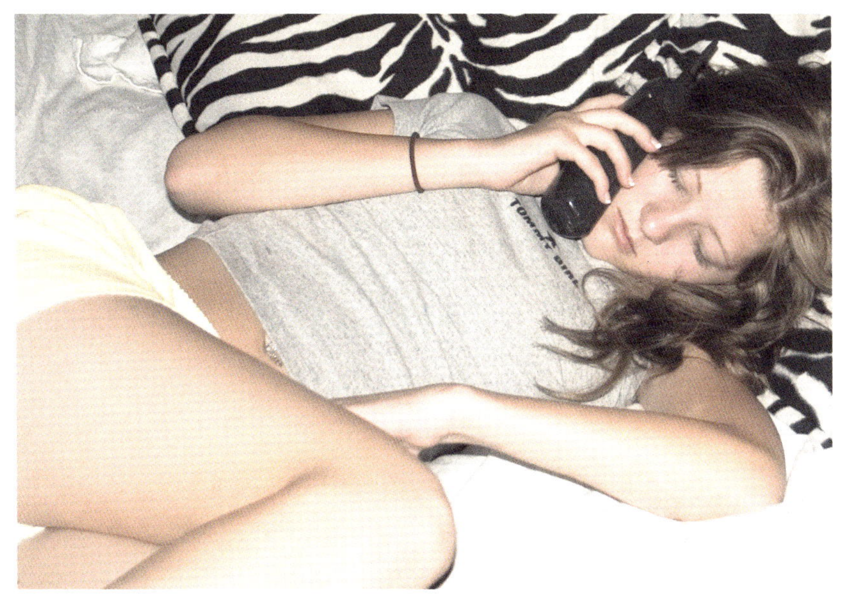

every hour in my America
beauty nibbles its split ends
in the fluorescent flicker
of an undisturbed thought
before the killing begins

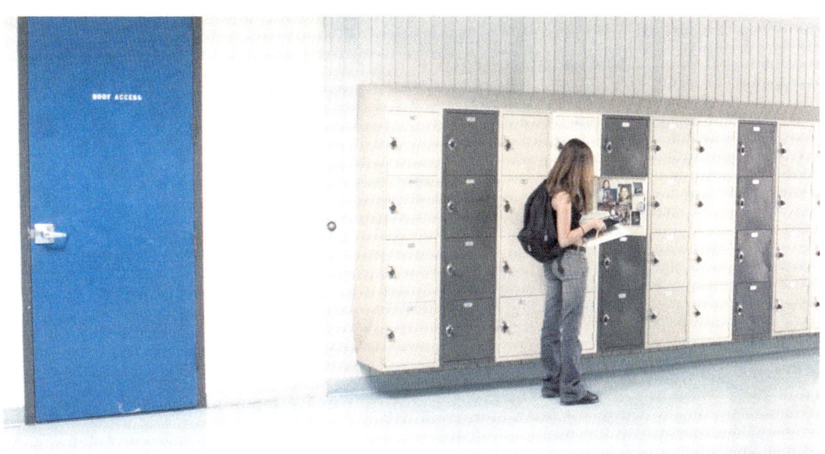

Over swingset, cul-de-sac, prison, racetrack,
Mother-love and coverlet end.

Desert hung with big bomb clouds, very
pink like my sister sleeps a hundred years

until some mister with a silver pistol–
or like mountains of bedazzled phones.

Death won't touch one cell of me,
not this year or the ever next.

I snuggle in time's nest and perfect myself–
no race riot/oil war/angel's horn

will disturb the fable in which I fix
the way they found her in the airforce field.

I didn't let fear win. I asked my dwarf protectors
to bring me his head, and after the vigil

we kicked it in. Someone slipped me the keys
to a gold Escalade. When I wake, I set the table.

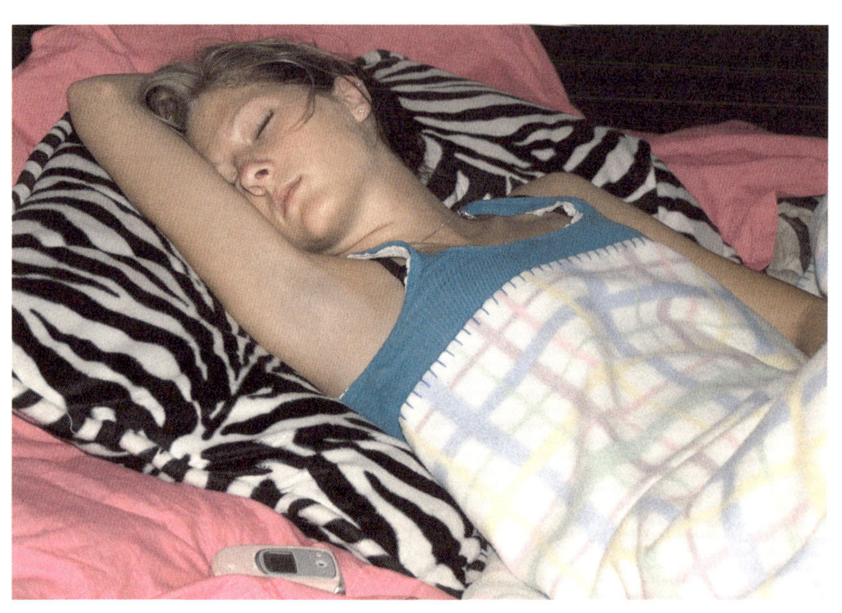

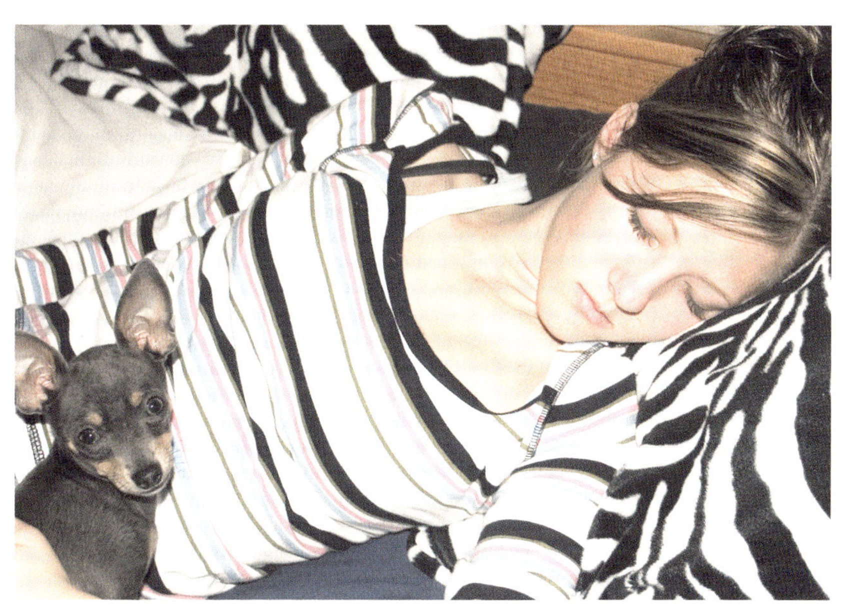

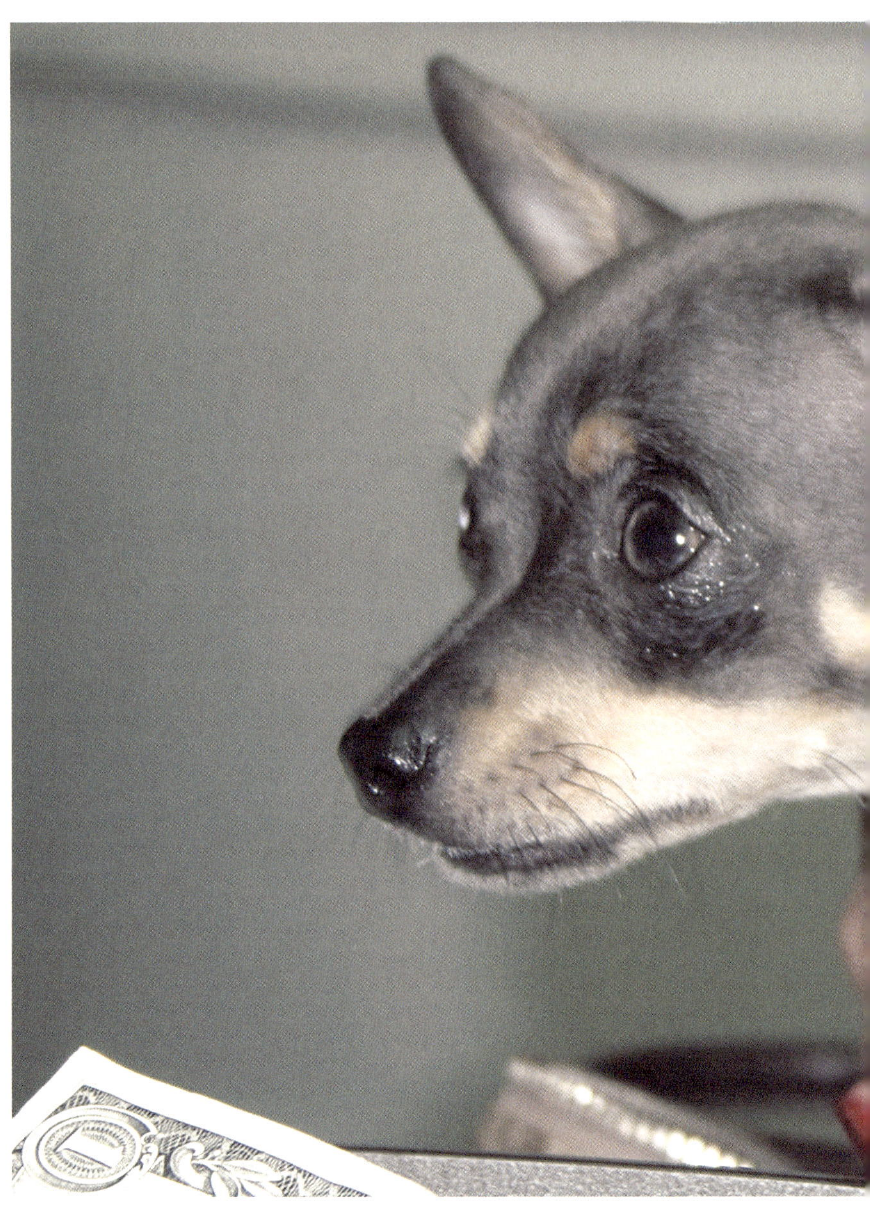

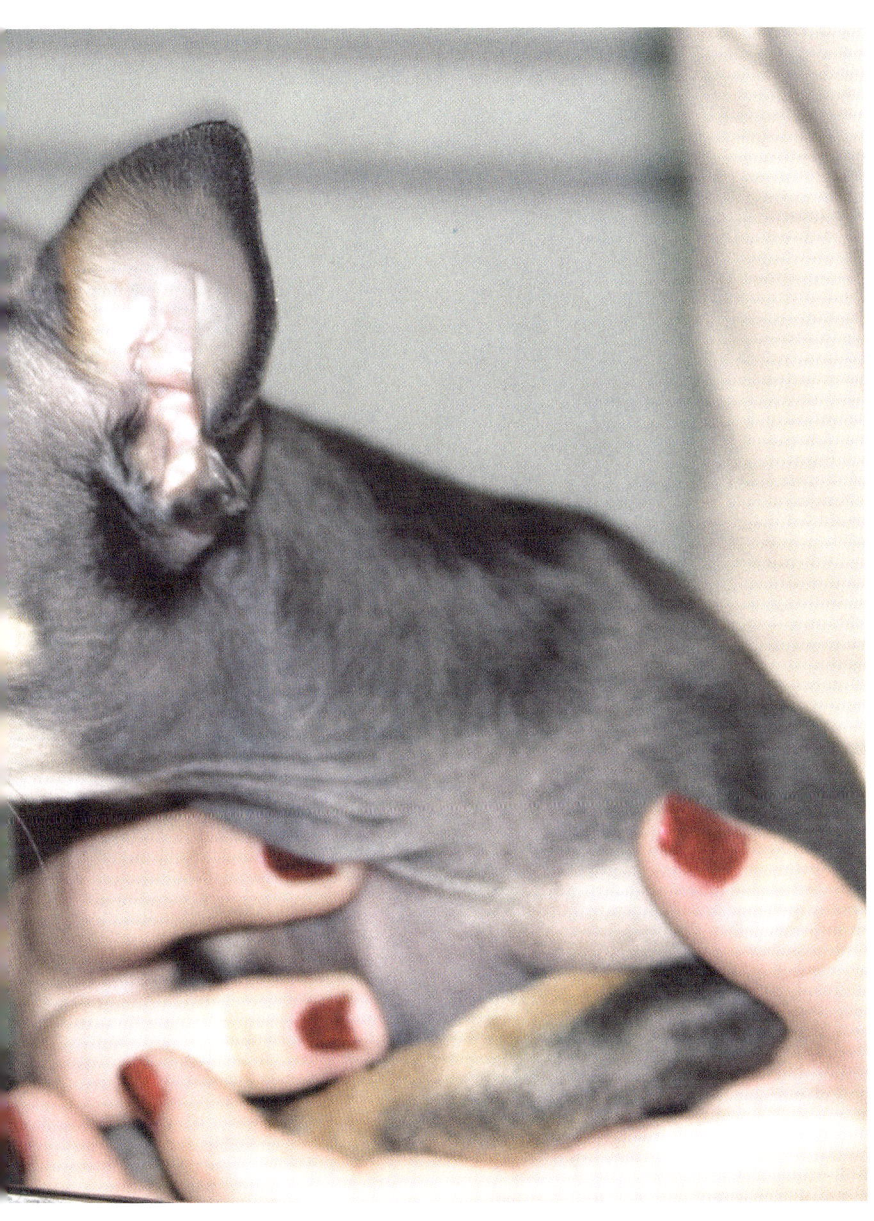

We get an address, an age,
a certain sun slanting over
our remarkable eyes
made new each moment
even in blurry youth
we begin by blinking
our first selves into being, live
by recalling almost nothing
except that day the world exploded
into shards of story we
feel like splinters
our full names written
in a list of survivors
when all we'd wanted
was to be the day's star.

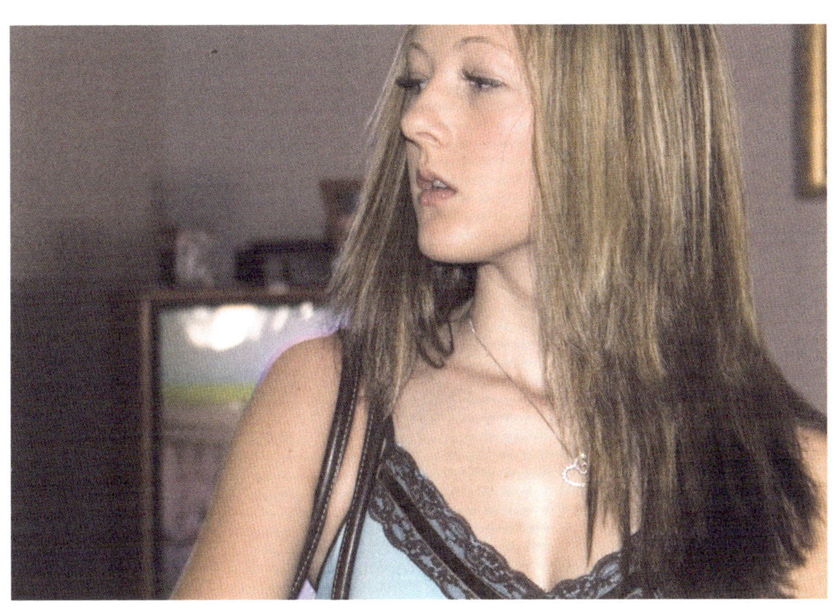

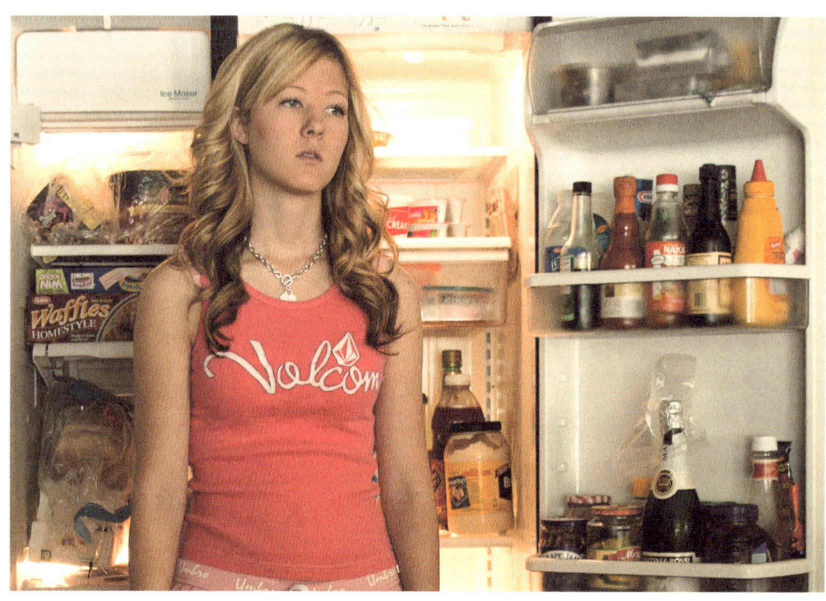
Ice Maker
Waffles
HOMESTYLE
Volcom

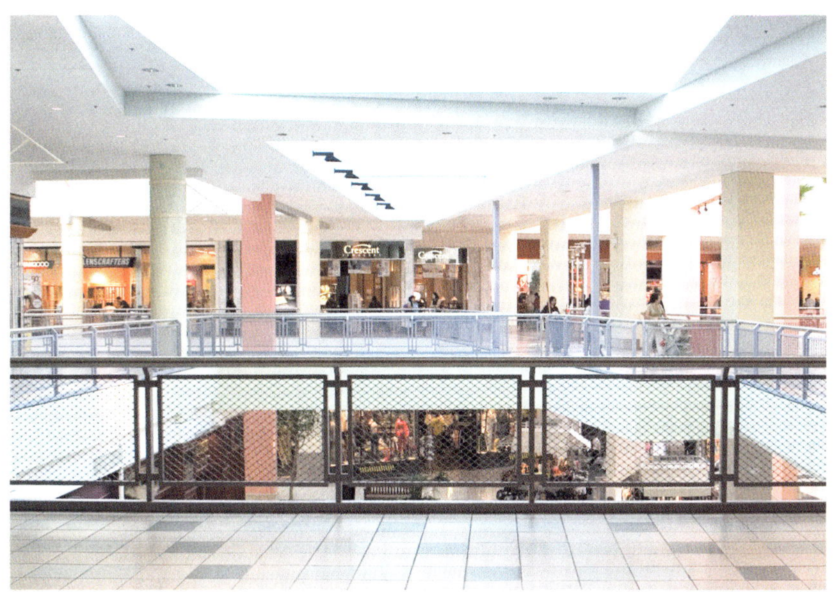
Crescent

The spirit exists
to kill us at hide-and-seek.

Red-winged blackbirds
make sad mascots
so bloody when we hang
our flag from high heaven

and stockpile canned peaches
in every fallout shelter
an eyelid's width
from god's cineplex

the spirit exists
to watch us believe.

A girl will hover at the edge
of herself, command each curve
speak its fresh dumb bloom,
grave beauty's drudgery
never more fluent.
We watch with rigor her
copy and improve a regular picture
in cold morning light
where god sees, too–
we watch a girl murder
her midnight mood
and better model a terrible care.
May the stars we're made of
take pleasure in their present glitter.
When she blinks, it shakes off
the last dust of us,
a piece of eternity
turns out real pretty.

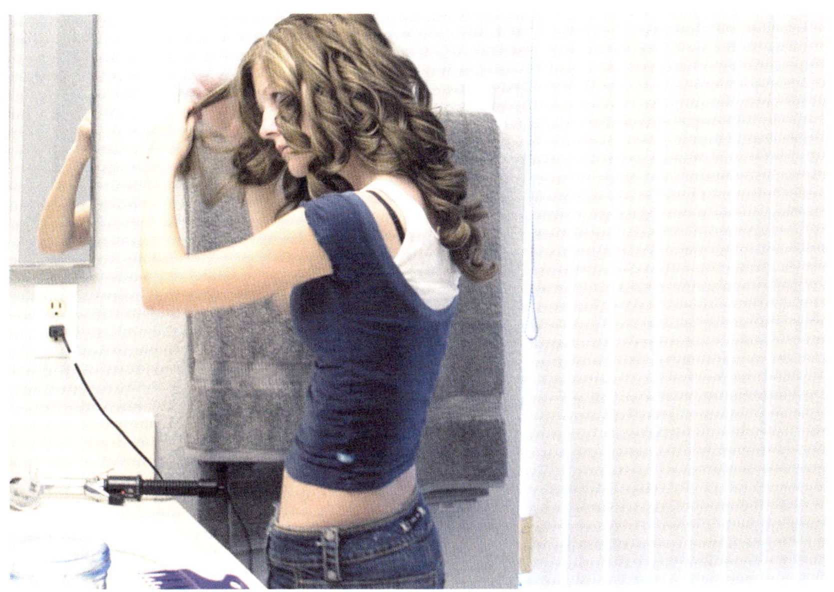

Praise all combustible stuff
that mingles in the landfill,
the songs that ghost the dead girl's
headphones, the ultrasonic sympathy
between the end of days
and this body I can briefly be
needs a trampoline to see
over tomorrow's earthquake drill.
I only reveal my brain tattoo
to the incandescent soul
of the one true listener, white moon
eyeing me just out of reach.
When I was born I knew all this
and more as one enormous bliss.

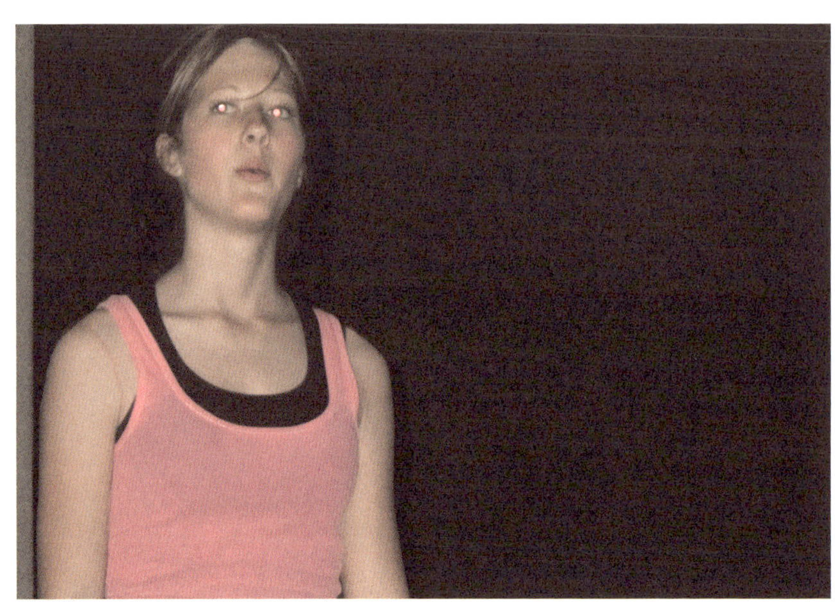

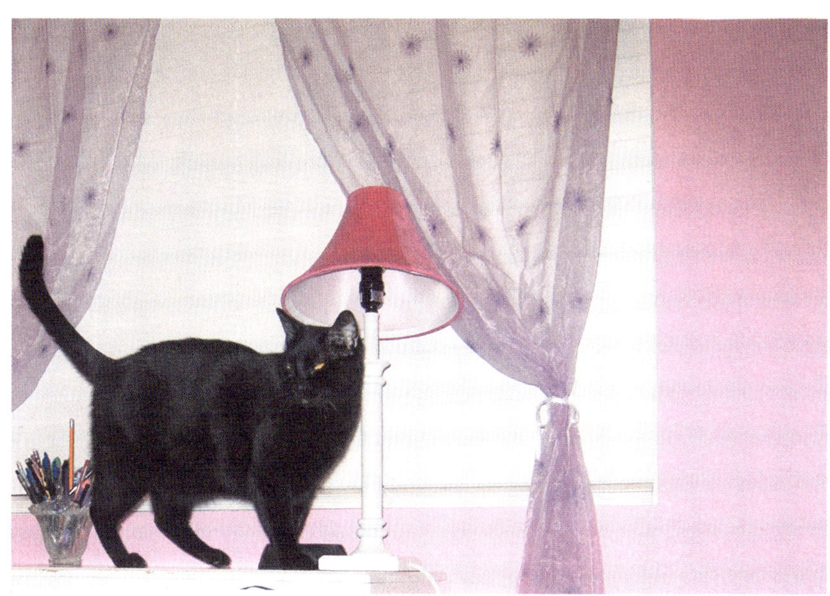

I could break or save you,
crack the sternum,
thrust your blood
with two laced hands
until you sputter her name.
Either way, I get paid.
No one can predict me.
I am not pregnant
with any known story, though mine
has the same alarm-clock pulse
as any payment-making daughter's.
Maybe stars still swirl above me.
Maybe I come from a concrete valley
and heart its man-made lakes.
Either way. Keys in a bowl by the door,
a balcony over the courtyard fountain,
a note to self to see the meteor shower.
I enlist no company to watch
the sun burn down behind me.

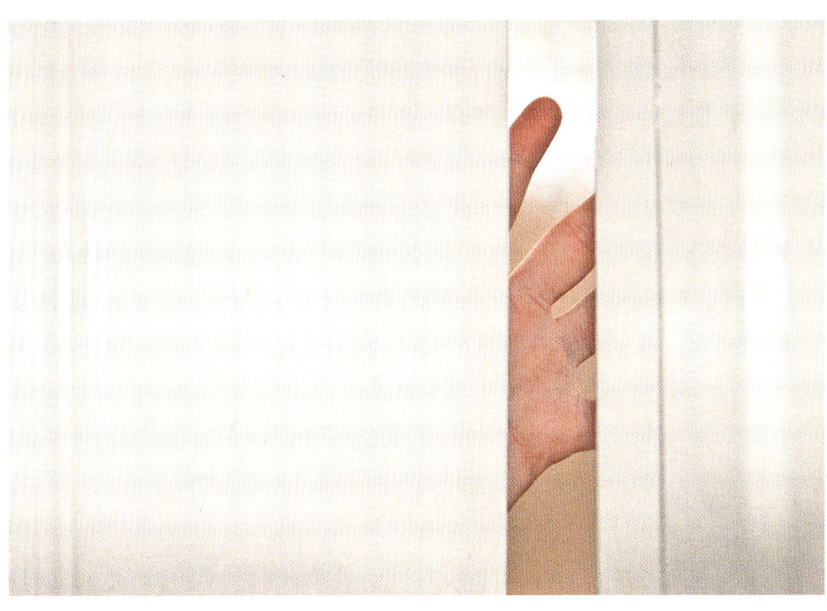

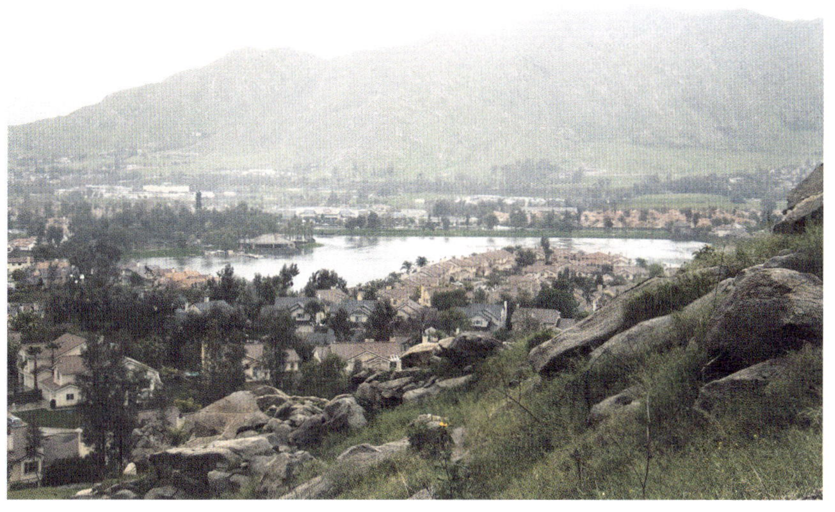

THE PHOTOGRAPHS IN THIS BOOK

WERE TAKEN IN MORENO VALLEY, CA,

FROM 2004 TO 2006 AS PART OF

THE CYRILLA STROTHERS PROJECT,

AN IN-DEPTH STUDY IN WHICH

FAMILY MEMBERS AND OUTSIDE OBSERVERS

RECORDED THE DAILY LIFE AND ENVIRONS

OF AN EXURBAN AMERICAN TEENAGER.

THE ACCOMPANYING POEMS WERE WRITTEN

IN LOS ANGELES, 2012, IN RESPONSE

TO THE SELECTED IMAGES.